Dwelling

Dwelling

poems

Allison Joseph

Red Hen Press | Pasadena, CA

Book design by Mark E. Cull

Library of Congress Cataloging-in-Publication Data

Names: Joseph, Allison, 1967– author.
Title: Dwelling: poems / Allison Joseph.
Other titles: Dwelling (Compilation)
Description: First edition. | Pasadena, CA: Red Hen Press, 2025.
Identifiers: LCCN 2025012249 (print) | LCCN 2025012250 (ebook) | ISBN 9781636283647 (paperback) | ISBN 9781636284347 (library binding) | ISBN 9781636283654 (ebook)
Subjects: LCGFT: Poetry.
Classification: LCC PS3560.O7723 D85 2025 (print) | LCC PS3560.O7723 (ebook) | DDC 811/.54—dc23/eng/20250424
LC record available at https://lccn.loc.gov/2025012249
LC ebook record available at https://lccn.loc.gov/2025012250

The National Endowment for the Arts, the Los Angeles County Arts Commission, the Ahmanson Foundation, the Dwight Stuart Youth Fund, the Max Factor Family Foundation, the Pasadena Tournament of Roses Foundation, the Pasadena Arts & Culture Commission and the City of Pasadena Cultural Affairs Division, the City of Los Angeles Department of Cultural Affairs, the Audrey & Sydney Irmas Charitable Foundation, the Kinder Morgan Foundation, the Meta & George Rosenberg Foundation, the Albert and Elaine Borchard Foundation, the Adams Family Foundation, the Riordan Foundation, Amazon Literary Partnership, the Sam Francis Foundation, and the Mara W. Breech Foundation partially support Red Hen Press.

First Edition
Published by Red Hen Press
www.redhen.org

ACKNOWLEDGMENTS

Poems from this collection were previously published in the following journals:

Atticus Review: "Ars Poetica With Lifetime Movie," "Letter to February," "Prayer to the Gods of Marriage"; *Cider Press Review:* "Letter to a Funeral"; *Dogwood: A Journal of Poetry and Prose:* "For Dinah Washington"; *ducts.org:* "Her Chair"; *Fledgling Rag:* "In Praise of Bugs," "Variation on a Line from Lorca," "What Jimi Told Prince, 1979"; *Southern Indiana Review:* "Tom: The Later Years"; *The Tower Journal:* "Encyclopedias," "To Lyric Poetry"; *Vox Populi:* "Elegy for Too Many"; *The Wide Shore:* "Nocturne With Awkward Dancing."

CONTENTS

Dwelling

ODE TO NOT DRIVING

I walk slow, walk fast, count steps,
make cars pause as I shuffle,
amble, creep, skip, dance
on the median, hustle and flow
as I make my way through this world

of exhaust and horns, headlights
and taillights. I don't know why
it's almost taboo to be a woman
without wheels, to trust my own
two feet and my faulty yet intriguing

sense of direction,
to walk and run and pedal
for my life, to have sixty second
dance parties down supermarket
aisles. It's bliss to ramble a country

lane, covered by a canopy of breathing
trees. It's bliss to be caught by a wave
of walkers headed out of Union Station,
bound for the city's most important
destinations, determined scowls

on their faces. Look down to behold
all those different shoes headed
somewhere, all moving in that
steady stream of limbs. How can you
not love the machine we all make

as we walk, marching for our lives,
our mothers' and our fathers' lives?
I think of my father-in-law,
how the Parkinson's took him
from elegant walker to hunchback

to chair bound to bedridden
to gone, and I know I must
walk now for him: head up,
feet forward, breath in my lungs,
body undeterred by traffic
jams, potholes, stoplights.

NOT THERE

That moment the world said
goodbye to you, cancer cancelling
your lungs for good, I was not there.

Not there when all the chemo,
all the radiation, all the prayer lists
and late night radio finally failed you,

failed my father—whom you called out to
in the hospice dark—singing his one-syllable
name—*Joe, Joe*—again and again.

Wasn't on a plane headed home,
not in a car or a train or in any way
getting closer to your bedside,

Not walking those pallid, pastel
hallways hoping for a miracle
beneath all those crosses.

I was busy being the girl,
the silly college girl,
you'd worked all those years

to let me be. So when I cried out,
when I knew you were gone, it was a cry
of failure, of a daughter no longer a daughter.

NOCTURNE WITH AWKWARD DANCING

What is it about nighttime that makes me
turn the music—any music—up way past
respectable to shuffle into the kitchen

to slide, reach, and bend, to pirouette
like a drunken ballerina? Something about
nighttime's hazy light and candlewicks

turns up my rhythms and down my
inhibitions, footsteps freer while the rest
of you snore and toss in sweaty bedclothes.

This dancing insomnia, this fitful 1-2 step,
gives me a kind of inflatable joy, fever
of visions and bare feet, toes clinging

to unwashed linoleum, arms flung out,
back, shoulders rolling forward. I'm
an unruly earthquake, unstopped geyser,

planet set loose from gravity, body giddy
with relief from shame's daily mandates.
Easier to sing and shimmy under invited

shadows, to be this untethered child
when the refrigerator's hum is all
the applause I need, or want. So if

you stumble upon me, spinning
like the world's worst dervish,
don't, I beg, turn on the light.

Leave me, body haunted by percussion,
to spin myself silly, turn myself out,
legs testing every motion daytime shuns.

AFTER A BAPTISM

They forced me in the water;
    they sank me in the sea.
Despite my wailing protest,
    they did what's best for me.

They took me to a chapel.
    They parked me in a pew;
they told me of the heavens
    but said only a few

of us were worthy people—
    the rest of us were damned.
I shook in clammy fear,
    the Bible in my hands.

I sang the sweetest hymns,
    my voice a sad refrain;
I knew that in their heaven
    I never could attain

the kind of peace they spoke of,
    an everlasting bliss.
I felt a sicker feeling,
    church bulletin in my fist.

I tried to be of faith,
    stilled questions in my mind,
But still the questions echoed,
    I had to be *that* kind.

I raised my hand to ask
    if God would follow me
if I ran from the chapel
    would He still want to be

Eternal Lord and Savior,
    the captain of my world.
But the preacher man ignored
    the way my spirit twirled

with agonizing doubt.
    He said, *just you believe,*
there's nothing more to say.
    But that did not relieve

the doubt I couldn't shake.
    No matter how I shifted
whenever I was there,
    my soul was never lifted.

I still sang all the hymns,
    I trembled in those pews.
And in my imperfections,
    I knew the faith I knew.

HER CHAIR

My mother must have been tired
of being mother, wife, some patient's
nurse, tired of a house of dust

and abandoned appliances
drained of their usefulness,
of house keys, doormats,

throbbing of my father's TV
and ringing telephone, his primitive
remote slipping beneath easy

chair cushions. Home from work,
seeing spilled toys, clothes, books,
my dolls with their dead faces,

why was she never tempted
to leave, seek quiet somewhere
besides our crumbling house

with its falling kitchen tiles,
gift-paper skeletons of past
Christmases, fossils of my father's

home improvements, his threadbare
underwear, soiled dress shirts, jeans?
Home from the hospital wards,

long shifts of tending and mending
strangers, didn't she have a right
to refuse us dinner, refuse us

everything? But she came home,
full grocery bags intact despite
her walk from the bus stop,

despite our bathroom clutter
of toothbrushes, washcloths,
kitchen with the broken-clock

oven, living room
with no recliner for her,
no easy chair for her hard work.

IN PRAISE OF BUGS

Who couldn't help but love your cross-dressing,
wise-cracking self, fruit crowning your head,
sarong around your non-existent hips, lips

pursed red and ripe for a juicy smack?
Street hustler, flim-flam bunny, weren't you
everyone's first drag queen? Able to tunnel

miles and miles underground, sitter
to baby-faced gangsters, you made everyone
look foolish—woodenheaded Elmer,

dopey hunter whose gun you tied in bows,
that neurotic duck who always thought
himself superior, though he never made

anyone laugh—that monster whose hair
you did—sticks of TNT for curlers.
Such an interesting monster, too,

you purred, right before you blew his
head off. You showed me so many
career paths—farm-wrecker, cowboy

thrasher, deviant from my own planet,
hare from round the block and who
knows where, carrot ninja, joker

jouster, sanest trickster this side
of Albuquerque. You taught me which
holes to pop out of, how to torment

my tormentors, how to ad-lib and
smack-talk, how to live the most
authentic life anyone could on a

Saturday morning. I'll forgive you
for falling for that girl bunny robot.
When the air is Disney-thick

and full of Smurfs, I'll adore
you forever. Anyone who loves you
knows life is what's up, and we

better live it loud and wild,
chomping down on everything
that doesn't bite us first.

ENCYCLOPEDIAS

Ripe with information, we once were
the center of everyone's living rooms,
proudly shelved to show the world

how smart each family was,
so many volumes spanning
countries, worlds, universes.

Every mother thought us necessary,
bought us on the installment plan,
book by book as a supermarket

promotion. We had our glory
years of solving family arguments
over state capitals and Miss America

winners. Now we're dumpster
dwellers, library castoffs,
Goodwill and Salvation Army

inmates, or left in basements
to rot and mold, no one caring
if floods leach ink from our pages.

No longer do sons and daughters
pour over us, thinking us book-report
worthy. Our city data and population

charts are out-of-date, we concede,
but our color photos still vibrate
all the spectrum's hues—images

of planets, moons, galaxies!
Won't you save us? When you claim
there's no room in your house

for us, you're saying there's no room
in your life for knowledge. Keep
your ignorance. Someone, somewhere

will love us, want to turn our pages,
because we know so much more
than any of you can remember.

AUBADE IN WHICH I ALWAYS RETURN

While you sleep, mask tethering you
to breath, machine pushing dreams into you,
past your body's reluctance to sink
into sacred REM, I lace up sneakers,
slip out our cluttered house's side door,

body and limbs waking into ache
as I start that morning's run, legs finding
their rhythm over sidewalk cracks and gashes
in blacktop, hips my true center of motion,
propulsion echoing with each footfall.

I've pledged these hips to you, and you
have loved them no matter their size,
amplification and diminution of flesh,
stretch marks lightly scoring my skin.
How brave it is to love a real woman,

cherish the stink of her sweat and hair,
unpainted face and chafed skin, rigor
of sunburn and windburn. And you have
loved me with constant courage, diligent heart,
encouraging miles that start in morning's

semi-dark, elusive hour of promise or failure,
growing light making plain stealthy shapes
or squirrels or birds, trees turning back
into trees from skeletal ghosts, shifting in
in irrepressible gusts. I let the miles collect,

trust in this body you have given
your trust, know you wait for me in your
assisted sleep, know when I stumble
out my last steps, turn the key in our house's
testy lock, you will ditch the mask,

rise to breathe on your own,
to hold these hips, this sore triumph
I only enact knowing I'll be back
for you to ask how I ran: how long, how far, how fast.

NIGHT WATCH FOR TRAVELING HUSBAND

Night feels thicker when you are gone,
heavier, full of deceptive shapes
and roaming cars that could be yours,

but aren't. I'm such a silly girl, waiting
for your return, cool patience of the long-
married replaced by bubbling anxiety,

shape-shifting tension unrelieved
by the madly barking dogs next door
who resume their frenzy anytime

any vehicle approaches. Should I
go to the window one more time,
peer through curtains one more time,

hoping you are off the highways
and at last onto local streets,
descending into neighborhoods

you know, coming around
the cul-de-sac, tires gliding
onto the driveway? Sleepless,

fretting, I know exactly how far
away you are, mark off miles on a
mind's eye map, know where

you will fill up or stop to eat,
but I still hope to see you
sooner than the speed limit allows,

damning any incident or accident
that clogs the interstate, any cop
with a quota to be made, any

construction site with vested
stop-sign workers. Night,
bring him back to me before

you tumble into day, before hated
sunrises and solo breakfasts.
Night, release him to my lair.

DWELLING

My pleasing company
comes wrapped in this brown skin—
my body's legacy
of history within.

I live in this brown skin,
my lips and this broad nose.
Of history within,
of bitter highs and lows,

my lips and this brown skin,
this hair and these brown eyes
have seen the highs, the lows—
I seldom feel surprise.

This hair. And these brown eyes
know all the brands of hate.
I seldom feel surprise
in neighborhoods with gates.

See all these brands of hate:
online or in a note,
in neighborhoods with gates.
No matter if I vote.

Online or in a note,
some minds refuse all change.
No matter if I vote
or if I rule the stage.

Some minds refuse all change,
refuse to listen well.
Though I might rule the stage,
they're getting prepped to sell.

They've ceased to listen well
to my body's legacy,
so quick to feel and sell
my pleasing company.

WOMAN WAITING

I'm waiting in the airport
    for the hour of redemption
    heavy baggage for the journey
        weighting me at the wrists
I'm waiting in the train station
    for a minute of consolation
    watching arrivals and departures
        with a tattered schedule
I'm waiting in the supermarket
    for a fraction of compassion
    briefest eye contact
        exchanged for my change
I'm waiting in the hospital
    for a sliver of insight
    all those numbers on my chart
        some headache I can't read
I'm waiting in the bus depot
    for a diagram of empathy
    some chart of all the routes
        to make a clean escape
I'm waiting in the alleyway
    for a gram of grace
    some bit of exaltation
        to keep me from my own throat
I'm waiting in the settlement
    for a flask of fantasy
    some deep draught
        I cannot help choke down
I'm waiting in the bathroom
    for an inch of lucidity
    some scrap of rest
        unknown to any mirror

I'm waiting in the orchard
    for a jigger of gratitude
    some split of land unfettered
        by the bruises of weather
I'm waiting in the graveyard
    for a flash, a siren, a signal,
    for confirmation this world
    is more than anticipation
    more than this mourning
    collapsing and unraveling
        never adding up
        to any proper weave

TOM: THE LATER YEARS

I spent so much time in pursuit
of a mouse I never really knew—
flash of fur and malice,

slapstick-silly and eager for
his blood. But sooner or later,
every cat feels a slowing

in his bones, explosions
and pratfalls adding up
to aches that do not fade

but magnify, landings on my
paws no longer a quick, graceful
scramble. I do not remember

why we tortured each other
year after year, decade after
decade, my noggin slammed

against holes he'd pop out of,
his mousy apartment inside,
with its matchbox bed, spool

for a table. Now when Jerry
comes, he comes with toys,
treats, a small saucer of milk,

leading me to it for my eyes
are cloudy disks, glaucoma-ridden.
I don't eat much anymore,

though I was once ravenous,
tense with running, full
of frenzied feline energy.

Now my limbs stiffen.
Now I take charity
from a mouse, my pride

in the chase replaced
by need, by failure,
the slow creep of impending

end, depending
on my enemy to lead me
to whatever's keeping me alive.

FOR DINAH WASHINGTON

Born poor, born colored, born Ruth Jones,
she had to become Dinah, had to show
that a tubby girl from the Tuscaloosa projects
could be queen, wear a tiara like nobody's
business, a slick chick on the mellow side,
making melodies behave when men didn't.
She brought gospel from the churches
to the clubs, sang blues behind her mama's
back to make cash money so they'd never
have to share a pair of stockings again,
changed her name to front jazz bands—
Hampton's, Lucky Thompson's All-Stars,
Tab Smith's. Think of her in furs, satin,
making a fool of Brook Benton on corny
duets like "Baby, You've Got What It
Takes." She complains at record's end:
You're in my spot again, mad he'd even
dare sing over her lines. Don't think of her
broken, broke, desperate from too much
drink and too many diets, too many one-
nighters, husbands—seven, eight, or nine,
depending on the bio. Don't think of her
as a maid's child, drifter's daughter, dead
from pills and booze. Think of her, gutsy
and bejeweled, salty and Southern on "Evil
Gal Blues," sultry-smooth on "What A
Diff'rence A Day Made." Think of her,
striking on stage at the Regal Theatre,
striding out there like she owned it, owned us.

WHAT JIMI TOLD PRINCE, 1979

Let all that electric music
send your hair to the sky,
fingers frenzied over frets.
You've got to make her
your religion—worshipping,
pleading, wringing her cries.
Down on your knees
if the out-of-body music
insists, her trance deeper
than drugs, groupies, freaks—
your every vision dislocated
in pursuit of holy rhythm,
burn of incendiary logic,
fiery feedback. I'm passing
all this heavy bluster
on to you, 'cause I know
you can handle these crucial
grooves, incantations of velvet
dissonance, scorching strokes,
glitter and love beads.
Headstrong, heartless kid,
savior of all Minnesota,
can't tell you nothing.
But I need to be a visitor
to your purple fever dreams—
your lusts my legacy,
your licks my soul.
When I first heard you,
I knew nothing could kill me.

CHANT FOR A NEW POET GENERATION

What's this strange relationship
between your sugar walls and mine,
glam slam of your legs, cream
of these holy hips? We gather here

dearly beloved, in purple, in heat,
around the block and around
the world, in a day, in seven
days—musicology of it all

turning us lovesexy, delirious
to the max. We are stardust,
we are golden—thieves in temples
we build from alphabet streets,

pearls beneath our tongues,
words diamond-hard.
The morning papers assault us
with far too many signs,

but we still rise though all
the critics don't love us,
never have. We keep moving,
one kiss at a time, our groove

under this nation, dance
music sex romance urging us
forward, profound as time,
as the jam of this

and every year.
Brothers and sisters,
friends and lovers,
each of us is symbol,
is slave, and we

are all funky,
our names a parade,
a housequake,
under the ripest moon,
cherry-red.

ENVYING THE GRANDMOTHERS

Because they are willing to rise at four a.m.,
drive to the airport and peel off their shoes
and cardigans to waddle through some
tiny airport's security line, I envy them.

No federal regulations will stop them
from seeing the seven-year-old
in Albuquerque, two-year old
in Boise, even the dazed seventeen-

year-old in San Diego. Cheeks must
be stroked, sweets snuck into
mouths that usually never get sugar.
Daughters-in-law must be scolded

then hugged, then scolded again,
sons-in-law must be taken down
as many pegs as needed for the
ultimate welfare of the grandchildren,

for they keep the grandmas living
despite dowager's humps and hips
shot through with arthritis, fingers
gripping canes, swollen cankles.

I want grandmotherhood
despite skipping motherhood,
want that undeniable tenacity
of affection, that full breath

and body shiver upon
receiving child-sized markers
of affection: sloppy kisses,
food-bearing fingerprints,

even the mumble-grumbles
of the teens, who are still
grandchildren despite all
the trappings of semi-adulthood—

learner's permits, college
brochures. The closest I get
is aunthood—an uncashed check
in a late birthday card,

a graduation announcement
the day after the ceremony.
Still, there are hard candies
in my purse for that one child

who won't mind having
an extra nana, gramma,
grandmommy—that kid
who finds my lap irresistible,

my wisdom irrefutable,
my arms wide enough
to fend off any world
that would bring my baby down.

LETTER TO FEBRUARY

The *bru* in you is brutal:
manic storms, guttural winds,
deluges of ice and harm,
dingy snow that lingers
long past white. It's not
lost on me that you
are an upgrade—a month
instead of "Negro History
Week,"—but the struggle
is realer on snow days,
my Caribbean blood
angry at sub-zero wind chills
and merciless montages
from arctic regions.
I propose we swap February
for June—after all, Juneteenth
needs the publicity, and we can't
all escape to the Bahamas
the second month of the year.
You are too short and mean
to honor any people's history,
and the fact that you make bills
due even faster makes me hate you
even more. So go home, February,
you're drunk on raging drifts
and blizzard smackdowns.
Sit down until we tell you to get up.

BOP: AUBADE WITH CHAKA

Another morning of bruised headlines
and who wants to think about rising?
All these death threats in invisible ink;
all these bomb threats easier to find
than rhyme schemes. Tell me something good
or turn it all off, all the air poised with spite.

you ain't got no kind of feeling inside

News bureaus shut down in the stutter
of a eye, slashed and murdered
reported left for dead on video.
We turn away, too tired for grief,
want goddesses to be goddesses
again. Territories drawn on maps
have no place in this constant drone
assault of visuals in each morning show.

you ain't got no kind of feeling inside

What salvation is there in screens,
in androids and tabloids? I only
find hope in one woman's funk
manifesto, manifest destiny of basslines
the only declaration I can dance to
waking up into this ceaseless dark world.

you ain't got no kind of feeling inside

PRAYER TO THE GODS OF MARRIAGE

I thank you each day for freedom
from the toxic spills of divorce, plagues
of confrontation and accusation
accosting couples I once thought so firm
I wrote poems in praise of their beds.

I thank you for the most amorous
of advances done in the least obvious
of ways, the most remote of places,
new coasts discovered with finger's flick,
lick of a neck, tongues softer now,

familiar in a language made new
by the surge and slippage of time,
those tides that capsize us sometimes,
leave us clinging to the rungs of our bodies.
I thank you for the better hotels

in which to dally in, love in, sleep in,
rat-traps of our young marriage
given way to double rooms or king
beds, more territory to roam in,
eventually find each other across

continents of hotel sheets, bunched
blankets. Gods, after hearing litanies
of agony from broken drunken husbands
and damaged-beyond-desperate wives,
thank you for choosing us to bear

happiness and sanity into the world,
the one couple in seven square miles
not squabbling over the remote or
the whiskey, in-laws and kids,
custody of the car and history

of the hurts. I thank them and I
thank the fallible glorious man
who wakes me, daily, from sleep—
lips giving me the slightest possible
kiss one can give to claim another.

WE NEVER HAD A BABY

No child will have our poor vision,
no girl—rawboned and gap-toothed,
no boy—truck-addled and bow-legged.
Is our love less than, not holy,

selfish or selfless? It takes more
than love to keep love alive,
couples splitting all around us
with a nasty thud, clatter

of lawyers' billable hours.
The couples ferry children
back and forth like cargo,
but we never boarded ship,

never wanted those dangerous
waters, marital cowards.
No couple should have kids
to prove they're a couple,

hurling their DNA into the gene
pool just because. What sense
does it make to blame us
for what we didn't want to hold,

scorn us for a lack
of progeny when you can't
tell love when you see it:
everyone greeting us

as strangers at
every hotel check-in,
servers always asking
if our check should be split.

SORRY (NOT SORRY)

Mistakes were made. Apologies were lost.
The requisite amount of shame poured down.
Somebody, certainly, will pay the cost.

We're sorry for your pain, blithe way we tossed
aside all your concerns. Forgive our frowns.
Mistakes were made. Apologies were lost.

We heard all your complaints. We told our boss,
and he told his—we've seen them both around.
Somebody certainly will pay the cost

for all the wrongs you've felt, for every cross
our mass of errors made you bear. We found
mistakes were made. Apologies were lost

in piles of paperwork, beneath the gloss
of more important mail, tossed on the ground.
Somebody, certainly, will pay the cost

for what you're going through, the huge exhaust
you're feeling at the way we've dragged you round.
Somebody, certainly, will pay the cost.
Mistakes get made. Apologies get lost.

ODE TO A BED

after Pablo Neruda

Oh messy hatch of blankets and letters,
you seize me midday, make me long for you
in the desolate hours I am away.

I hide in you like an unruly schoolkid,
savoring snacks I perch high on pillows
so worn my head's indent makes them

like brothers to me, embracing my
hard noggin, sliding me into slumber.
The man I share you with is restless

and turns so heavily in his machined
sleep I almost blame you for it, then
remember we picked you out together,

choosing you from among all others
in the showroom's dazzling light.
We buy more and more blankets

for you, holding winter off you,
shedding layers months later,
cooling you from swelter.

We dress you in royal blue fitted sheets
because you are worth it—regal, rich,
relevant. We eat in the folds of those

sheets and blankets, propped on the rise
of pillows, feast where you let us feast,
embraced by all your nightly tidal motions.

THAT POEM YOU WROTE

Sprawled in the back
of some shady sedan,
that poem you wrote
is dating someone else,

stray syllables spread
all over that leather
interior, loose phrases
lounging untethered,

naked, bursting to be
anyone's but yours.
That poem you wrote
wants a refund, rebate,

a return to its previous form
where you doted on every
line, proudly clucking
on its beauty, its curvaceous

lineation. That was before
you hacked its heart
and called it revision,
before you slashed and cut

instead of gently shaping
and cooing. Your poem
slipped out while you slept
slack-mouthed, not suspecting

that what your words wanted
was the easy hook-up,
backseat groping. The only
way to make your poem

come crawling back, sad-eyed
and sorry for having left—
is to write a new poem,
a brand-new darling

bodacious with metaphor
and meaning, brimming
with beauty, a poem so
brilliant your old poem

will run back to stand outside
your door in the rain, bawling
for the comfort of your familiar
pen, your haughty headspace.

NOW NOT LATER

Don't wait until I'm dead to celebrate
my life, my words, the clever things I said,
my small indignities, my loves, my hates.
Don't weep for me; rejoice instead.

Recall the ways my appetite was fed:
strong wines, good sex, full plates
of pasta, all sauces, white and red.
Don't wait until I'm dead to celebrate

the days I walked this earth. Don't wait
until my sense of taste is dead,
those days when disability is fate.
My life, my words, the clever things I said—

relive them now, keep them inside your heads
to use when I'm disconsolate,
too tired to get out of bed.
My small indignities, my loves, my hates,

the qualities I don't appreciate,
remind me of it all. The life I've led
won't help me when it's grown too late.
Don't weep for me. Rejoice instead

when I am gone, no longer wed
to flesh and breath. Think of the date
I die, but not with tears or dread,
with joys that don't disintegrate.
Don't wait.

KNOWLEDGE IS POWER

Let me tell you what I know about blackness,
the older white man says to me, smiling graciously.
He's filling me in on me, learned and tactless,

reveling in his grasp of history,
with elegance and wisdom he must share.
The older white man says to me

it's not about your Afro, your thick hair,
Your problems are much bigger than your scalp.
With elegance and wisdom he must share,

he lectures me about the income gap
between blacks and whites, says I must do my part.
Your problems are much bigger than your scalp,

I want to see you tackle them in art!
He makes me savior, claims I have a gift.
Between blacks and whites, I'll try to do my part,

by tuning out his voice , his words adrift.
He's filling me in on me, learned and tactless.
He makes me savior, claims I have a gift.
Let me tell you what *I* know about: Blackness.

SOME PEOPLE

Some people think I'm clever;
some people think I'm not,
I never argue with them,
this mind is all I've got.

Some judge me to be pretty;
some frankly call me plain.
I think I'll split the difference,
not make myself insane

with questions about beauty,
and worries about looks.
I'd rather lavish love on words
and cultivate some books.

Some people find me mouthy;
some people claim I'm shy.
I flip my switch between those modes
and do not question why

I'm talkative at midnight
and sullen when I rise.
Some people prefer silence;
some people prefer lies—

I only want the kind of truth
that stings me in the eyes
and grabs some hidden part of me
to strip it of disguise.

Some people want to change me;
some people leave me be.
I only want to live a life
where I don't have to flee

from being elemental,
essentially this self.
Some people will not faze me
with their advice and wealth.

I'll listen to some people,
Some people, not at all.
I'll stop and hear your message
but won't be in your thrall.

Some people will ignore you.
Some people know your name.
I only want to breathe and write,
no need for the acclaim

that people stress and strive for,
that people want and crave.
I only want successive breaths
to keep me from my grave.

THINGS GIRLS HEAR

You should smile more—you'd be
so much prettier if you smiled.
And what's with your hair?
You should straighten it,
then curl it, then brush the curls
so they look natural. And speaking
of natural, you should wear makeup,
just a bit of it—bring out your eyes
more, which are beautiful by the way,
except maybe you should—and I
say this out of love—get those
colored contacts everyone's
talking about. You could try
blue eyes or hazel eyes and
all you'd have to do is put them in
everyday—no trouble at all.

You should definitely dress
a little better—I mean, you've
got a great body—why not show
it off, let people know what
you're working with? You
should wear skirts. Or dresses.
But not those dresses that look
like they're made with little
girls in mind—what are they
called—baby dolls? Yeah,
not for you—they'll just make
you look fat when you aren't,
and that's no good, isn't it?

You should wear heels
sometimes—I mean, if
you're going to wear dresses,
then you shouldn't wear sneakers
with them, unless you are wearing
a suit and just wearing sneakers
before you get to your job.
It's okay then, I suppose.
But if you're going to wear
a dress or a skirt to a bar,
then at least have the decency
to wear a pair of heels,

it looks so much nicer that way,
and you do want to look nice,
don't you? Sure, we all do—
even guys—they just don't know
it yet. And you should really
think about a good bra,
some white strips for those teeth,
some earrings and jewelry—but
no nose stud or belly ring,
and some nail polish, since no one
likes naked hands. You should
be good to go then, and no one
will be able to resist you, you vixen!

ARS POETICA WITH LIFETIME MOVIE

My beloved husband says, no poems
about poems, declaring them as useful
as rhubarb, which was a plot device
in a horrendous made-for-TV movie we watched

instead of writing poems about poetry, which,
I argue, can be fruitful and necessary,
unlike this movie which would have viewers believe
the sweater-wearing professor next door

is actually a sick psychopath with a hidden
bunker of kidnapped women beneath
his suburban ranch-style house. This plot,
I assert, is far less plausible than your

average ars poetica—which, at least,
might possess subtle word play and glistening
imagery. In this movie, which we watch
aghast at its Mack-truck-sized plot holes,

our friendly neighborhood psycho professor
chloroforms his hunky neighbor's fiancé,
forces her to swap her Portlandia threads
for the crinolines and lipstick of a 1950s

sitcom housewife. They carve a lot
of roasts in his hidden bunker,
which is protected by a security system
no untenured essay-grader could afford.

Anyone can afford an ars poetica though,
I maintain—a few lines, a turn of phrase
or two, some shuddery slither of insight
for an ending. By the time this movie

is done, there are multiple dead bodies,
the rhubarb has become pie, the prof's
languishing in prison, and the hunky
dude's fiancé has penned a tell-all

about her ordeal. It will be seen by more people
than will ever read this poem. But I declare
this poem has reason to exist, if only
to warn you of the time-suck of Lifetime movies.

I should be happy the psycho prof
wasn't also a poet, pleased he wasn't
quoting Randall Jarrell or lamenting the decline
of New Criticism. Small mercies do exist,

as do poems, as do poems about poems,
and I don't need a stint in some knife-wielding
anti-Modernist's basement to ward off all
the darkness above, all the pastel chaos.

LETTER TO A FUNERAL

Shouldn't you happen in winter, endless cold snap,
bitter winds bruising my chapped
cheeks? In movies, you are always gray,
set in misty graveyards where actors say
unsatisfying truths about life, death,
wandering between fake headstones left
out in the gloom of cinematic rain.
Unseemly to sweat through pain,
to bury our dead as unremitting sun
makes black dresses and ties cling
to our sodden mourning frames.
This lush sense of loss is better tamed
when cast-off leaves crunch beneath our feet,
when chimney smoke and pots of tea come sweet
enough to conquer grief, at least
for just a little while. Shouldn't mourning
wear a winter coat, a scarf, awnings
bowed with the season's first snow?
Your funeral should have been October,
November—season cold enough for embers,
for the burnt ends of fires we built
to warm us when the sun's tilt
turned away from us, left us cold,
but somehow better equipped for the old
songs of grief, songs of loss—
music sustaining us though we're tossed
by all of these arrangements, what they cost.
Still, it doesn't matter when the mourning's done.
In the heat, we're silent. We've come undone.

ELEGY FOR TOO MANY

Bring back the poets, all gone too soon.
Bring back Jake and Rane and Deborah and Reetika.
Bring them all back because reading their words is not enough
On a cold and darkening November day,
Where the temperatures will drop beyond comprehension.
Bring back Sarah, Rachel, Diane and Craig, back from the lows
And heights of despair, bring them back to breath,
To heartbeat and sigh, to write and give us sly smiles
From podiums they will not read from again.
Give them back to us intact, no fury but in rhythms,
No darkness but in ink. Give them back to us,
Brains not short-circuited by hemorrhage,
Hearts not slashed by chemistry, hands
Busy with the industry of typing, language
Firing cells, cerebral and celebrated.
Give me back their voices of ravishment,
Of terrible truths sung in the least of circumstances,
Sustenance for the faltering hours, the dimming light.
I want them all back from the bodies that
Failed them. I want them back, waving from
That distant shore of forgetfulness, walking
Back to the embraces I didn't get to give them.
I want them here, packing suitcases for a trip
That will have them see me at the airport
Right as we ready to board, slim books
For the journey in all our palms.

ODE TO AN UNLOVED TOWN

Cairo, Illinois

Tucked at the bottom of this unkempt state,
neglected by the governor's latest silence,
your mansions sit, bleak reminders
of the money once held in back room

bank vaults. Few tourists visit this
heartsore town, black and white turned
back into the segregated South, though this
is Illinois, state of Lincoln's justice,

of wealth and cul-de-sacs, private homes.
Here in Cairo, the last grocery store
has closed for good, the health clinic's
only open one day a week, as if pain

has a mid-week schedule, on time
every time. Every child here wants
to grow up, not return, sailing as soon
as a souped-up car and a license

make it so. People die here for want
of doctor, could lie in the center
of the roads as if wanting to be crushed
but so few trucks rumble their way

through here to the interstate—
no produce for the long chill ahead.
Churches still hold their mighty
doors open though—solace

in the winter, sustenance
in the summer, brick refuges
of hope when prisons make martyrs
of this town's men. Even the liquor

stores have bars on their windows;
even the schoolteachers
are on perpetual strike,
and no one wants to look closely,

as if poverty is catching, a fatal
disease. The one good thing
anyone claims here is barbeque,
but smoke and sauce and meat

can't keep a town alive,
keep a man from finding himself
on the riverbank, deciding
whether or not, at this lowest

point in Illinois, to jump
in where the confluence
of waters turn from blue
to brown, and back again.

HUMMINGBIRDS

for my father-in-law, gone three months

Tremors in his body did not quit,
evolved into paralysis, stasis
unkind to all his previous life,

familiar motions shrunken, gone,
words seized in his throat.
If there is a heaven, let him rise

from that bedridden body to
its peaceful halls and corridors,
its light and joyous passages. If

there is a heaven, let him walk
and taste again, its very air sweet
as the nectar his hummingbirds

sipped from the slender glass feeder
pendulous outside the sunny
window. This world I see before me

is a trap, a shame, flavors gone
for him. Each day another fight
to live, breathe, swallow.

Please. Let the joy of quick wings
surge him again, send him beyond
my tepid and timid understandings.

AT LAST: A BLUES PARADELLE FOR ETTA JAMES

All this hard luck loving's been rough on me.
All this hard luck loving's been rough on me.
Strung out, flat busted, I nearly lost my mind.
Strung out, flat busted, I nearly lost my mind.
Hard luck loving's been rough on me, my mind
strung out. Flat busted, I nearly lost all this.

My voice has aged from a girl's to a woman's.
My voice has aged from a girl's to a woman's.
I can get right down to a song's heart now.
I can get right down to a song's heart now.
My voice has aged right, from a girl's to a woman's.
Get down to a song's heart? I can now.

Come a little closer, let Etta heal your blues.
Come a little closer, let Etta heal your blues.
Remember, you can leave your hat on.
Remember, you can leave your hat on.
Remember, you can heal your blues.
Let Etta come a little closer. Leave your hat on.

I remember all this hard, strung out luck.
Busted loving's been flat rough on me, from a girl's
to a woman's. Let Etta heal. Aged, my voice
has a song's heart now. Nearly lost, I can
get right down to my mind, your blues.
Come a little closer. You can leave your hat on.

ON THE WAY TO THE ONCOLOGIST

They remind me of my in-laws, this pair—
him with tall gray head, oxygen can,
her with her unsteady gait, wispy hair.
It's a task for them to board the shuttle van,

the step up onto the vehicle a climb
her body's barely capable of making—
a height I skip up in no time
causes her to stop, swollen legs aching

as she tries to heave them up.
Her hands cling to the seats, the floor,
her husband behind her, ready to cup
her body should she fall, moving a chore

she says she can't abide. *No fun
getting old*, she says, as I reach out
to help her on. Her husband's done
this many times before, I have no doubt—

he's gently playful, stern—all at once.
They're going to St. Louis, not for fun,
not for grandkids' smiles or silly pouts,
but so doctors can poke and prod, run

all those blasted tests she's come to fear,
the nosy nurses and the waiting rooms,
the probing and the questions she can't hear.
They ask me if I'm married, then assume

my parents are among the living still,
though cancer took my mother long ago,
and diabetes killed my father's will
to live. It takes me several seconds to say *no,*

I miss them very much; they're not alive.
The silence settles in, as do the miles.
Why does it always take a lifetime to arrive
at the airport; why do my fake smiles

fail me when a strange pair cuts me quick?
They wave me gone, the van pulling away
to take them to those hallways for the sick,
aisles I'm sure will welcome me some day.

"NEWBORN CRY STIRS DYING MOTHER FROM COMA, FAMILY SAYS"

—KSL.COM, 9/16/15

Love is the longest sleep, the coma
that kept me from you until
I was ready to be a mother,
ready to wake and welcome you

with arms fits to hold, eyes
fit to see. You startled me
into my lungs again, plangent
cry tricking my heart into rousing,

thumping out of barest quietude
into full-throttle life. I don't
know what to call you: Lily
or Lucy, Regina or Alice,

little queen or soft soul,
diary of my thumbprint,
code of your father and me.
Little wit. Little darling.

Daring me to rise from this bed,
resist the monitor and feeding tube.
Angel made flesh, messenger
and passenger, your voice

will wake me so many more
times, shake me to my roots
when I'd rather slip back
into dreams that do not end.

You spurred me from that trance,
that spell, made me depart that
forsaken space, that gleam
of a starless planet, godless galaxy.

TO ALL THE CLOCKS I'VE KILLED

Sorry little timepieces all in a row,
some on my shelves and some
in a box, all dead now to time,
all stopped hands and frozen

digits. Forgive me for handling
you like you were nothing,
for knocking you down,
smashing you up, neglecting

your need for batteries,
leaving you in hotel rooms,
battering the ones in hotel
rooms, leaving you in closets

so the maids don't know
I took you down. I've
pitched you like softballs,
swept you off end tables,

hurled you, hurt you,
left you to die without
winding you or plugging
your frayed cords

into overtaxed outlets.
When I die, I hope
I am treated better
than this triage, this

hatchet job, this
ignorance of sacrosanct
minutes and seconds,
mutilation of hours.

PRODUCE AISLE

Abundance on the daily;
on sale and three
for a dollar, succulent

or seedless, pink flesh
under leathery rinds,
red delicious and

honeycrisp, a gala
of color on permanent
display—hot, tart,

and ripening. Globes
we can hold in public!
Shapes we can grab

with impunity!
Nibble on a few
grapes—don't get caught—

stash a few cherries
in my pocket! And oh,
that moment the mister

turns on, spraying
all those leafy, prickly
vegetables, our hands

damp over the kale
and spinach, fingers
slick on all that tasty

green, all that new money!

TO LYRIC POETRY

You mercury-slippery river
of reason, you blithe and bitter
heat under my bedclothes.

I'm stuck over in the tundra
of consequence and plot,
thumbing through old

newspapers for the truth,
fingers sticky with flop
sweat and chip dust.

But I am persuaded
by your nervous elegance,
your lean lines, your staccato

brevity pinging the shaky
heart I claim as mine.
I want to live inside your

vertigo, spinning and
spinning until I fall
at your feet, unspooling

all my ignorance
and grit. But I fear
the feeling of no

net below, suspended
in a harness always
threatening to give way.

LETTER TO MY TWELVE-YEAR-OLD SELF

So roughly beautiful, so sad-sack
skinny and wrong-way awkward,
you fear everything and anything,

all elbows and acne, stutter-thick
glasses and heat-rash haloes,
stubble of new hair in old

places. No diva, princess, model,
you finger holes in derelict
denim, pray aloud to the grand

god of puberty to bless you
with a desired body, breasts
high atop your chest, curves

haunting hips and the plain
blank spaces of your limbs.
You can't see anything but

your own ugly—braceface teeth,
church-knob knees, untamed hair
no chemical can fix. And I could

be kind, tell you one day you'll
be married, needed, safe,
you'll be valued for that mind

and that wit, all the physical
ceasing to matter, never a
tantrum in a clothing store,

never a diatribe after another
cover, glorious in celebrity Photoshop,
lands in your lap, in your mail.

But this is what you must know—
there will be fat days, bloat
days, sweat stains, indescribable hairs

in every wrong niche, will be
riches of embarrassments,
rip-offs of hormones, rigors

of weeks where everything
you touch gains the power
to make you that much smaller.

There will be limbs you'll lust for,
legs that will scurry away
just as you confess, you left

with all that ache and nowhere
to shove it. Your body will feel
like a house, a store, vacant lot

where carjackers abandon
burnt-out wrecks. But it's still
your body—fat, thin, old, young,

indifferent, in pain or bliss.
Those doubt-bitten lips? Yours.
Those glands spitting out drama?

Those passion plays of breath?
All yours. I could try to tell
you different, but that would

make us both liars, and no one needs
another liar, not you—caged-tooth warbler,
not me—middle-aged prophet.

VARIATION ON A LINE FROM LORCA

If I am dying, leave
the back door open.

Let the neighborhood strays
wear their fur around

each ankle, claws unhidden.
Let my house collapse,

grow lush in neglect:
trees and bushes thick,

tangled as the bramble
of my midnight hair,

damaged as my terrified
legs. When the sun rises,

I'll know the calm breath
God never sent, know

the missing digits of his
last known address,

wrecked by the soil
of all his unspeakable graves.

BIOGRAPHICAL NOTE

Allison Joseph lives in Carbondale, Illinois, where she is on the faculty at Southern Illinois University. Her most recent collections of poems are *Lexicon* (Red Hen Press, 2021, PBTS Best Book Award winner), *Any Proper Weave* (Kelsay Books, 2022), *Speak and Spell* (Glass Lyre Press, 2022), and *Confessions of a Barefaced Woman* (Red Hen Press, 2018). *Confessions of a Barefaced Woman* won the 2019 Feathered Quill Book Award and was a finalist for the 2019 NAACP Image Award. She was named Illinois Author of the Year for 2022 by the Illinois Association of Teachers of English. Her poems have appeared in the *New York Times* and in the *Best American Poetry* Series. She is the widow of beloved poet and editor Jon Tribble.

www.ingramcontent.com/pod-product-compliance
Lightning Source LLC
Chambersburg PA
CBHW031148090426
42738CB00008B/1263

* 9 7 8 1 6 3 6 2 8 3 6 4 7 *